Antler on the Sea

The Anthropology of Contemporary Issues

A SERIES EDITED BY

ROGER SANJEK

A list of titles in this series is available at www.cornellpress.cornell.edu.

career courage